BIBLE READING

HANDBOOK

Paul Schuessler

Augsburg Fortress, Minneapolis

Contents

Acknowledgments

Design: Garry Gamble

Scripture quotations are from the Holy Bible, New International Version, copyright © 1973, 1978, 1984 International Bible Society. Reprinted by permission of Zondervan Bible Publishers.

ISBN 0-8066-2586-4

1 2 3 4 5 6 7 8 9 0 1 2 3 4 5 6 7 8 9

Introduction

A third-century church leader wrote, "Our souls are restless until they find their rest in God." Augustine easily could have described our souls as "hungry," hungry for God. No doubt Jesus understood the hunger for a relationship with God, and that is why he called himself the Bread of Life. We can come to know God and God's Son, Jesus, and be nourished by reading God's Word, the Bible. Through regular study of Scripture, we *will* be fed.

As valuable and exciting an experience as reading the Bible can be, many people hesitate to attempt it because they do not know where to begin. Perhaps they also are overwhelmed by the sheer size of the Bible, and they suspect they will not understand it.

This handbook to the Bible will help you decide what to read and point you to resources that will help you understand what you read. Often, people find that the best way to read the Bible is to follow a selective path, rather than to read it straight through from beginning to end. *Bible Reading Handbook* maps out a path through Scripture. And it will show you how to chart your own route so that you can retrace your steps or branch out as you read.

There is a story in the Gospel of Luke (Luke 24:13-35) about two disciples traveling on the road from Jerusalem to the town of Emmaus. It was the first Sunday after Jesus had been crucified and laid in a tomb. The disciples were joined by

Jesus along the way, but they did not recognize him. The mysterious traveler seemed not to know what had been happening in Jerusalem the last few days, and the two disciples eagerly told him about the amazing events that had taken place. And then Jesus, without revealing who he was, interpreted all that the Scriptures said about him.

It was not until later, when the two ate a meal with Jesus, that their eyes were opened and they understood why their hearts were burning within them when they listened to Jesus. They finally saw who Jesus was.

As you walk through Scripture and hear for yourself what God has done for us, your eyes also will be opened, and you will come to understand why Jesus called himself the Bread of Life.

1 Why Read the Bible?

When Jesus asked God to help his disciples carry out their mission in the world, he prayed, "Sanctify them by the truth; your word is truth" (John 17:17). He used the word *truth*, not in the scientific sense we might first think of, but to mean that God's Word is reliable. It can be counted on. We can count on the Bible to answer three basic questions of life:

The question of faith: Who needs God?

The question of hope: How can I carry on?

The question of love: Who really cares?

Once you begin to explore Scripture, you will discover that there are many reasons to read the Bible. People have found reading the Bible inspiring and helpful in order to:

- Learn to know God and understand God's will for them.
- Allow God's Word to help them understand themselves better.
- Find strength and comfort in times of distress, illness, or grief.
- Develop a more meaningful prayer life.
- Share their faith with others.

Jesus himself relied on the Scriptures throughout his life to validate and inspire his ministry. He even prayed from the Psalms during his crucifixion. Jesus knew that he could count on Scripture because it is *God's* Word, and we can count on God. We can count on God to care for us, to nurture us. When we read the Bible, God loves us through the Word. God feeds us with the Word.

2 How to Choose a Bible

If you do not own a Bible, or if you want to buy a new one, you will quickly discover when you go to make your selection that there are dozens of editions from which to choose. The most important choice to consider is the translation you will use.

The Old Testament originally was written in Hebrew, the New Testament in Greek. Translations of the Bible are necessary so that God's Word can be preached, taught, confessed, believed, and shared in languages all people can understand.

But why are there so many translations or versions of the Bible?

Translations are made from ancient manuscripts that were handwritten on various materials. Most of the manuscripts available to scholars are in poor shape—they are torn or have holes in them. Or only small pieces, perhaps a few inches or less square, have survived. Few Old Testament manuscripts exist. Portions of over 5000 New Testament manuscripts exist, but except for minor fragments, the oldest are from several hundred years after Jesus lived, and no two manuscripts agree exactly.

However, biblical scholars continue to study the manuscripts available, and manuscripts, some in good condition, continue to be found, so translations can be improved gradually. In addition, archeological discoveries have made it possible for us to know more about the world of the Bible and to understand customs and verify facts that were once mysterious. Newer translations reflect these archeological findings.

New translations also are prepared because the English language changes over time and from one place to another. Words that once were accurate translations of the Hebrew and Greek Scriptures might be misleading now. New translations avoid language that could be misunderstood.

To help you choose a Bible, here are descriptions of the best known English versions of the Bible in use today.

The **King James Version** (KJV) is also called the **Authorized Version** (AV) because King James of England authorized it in 1611. The translation was available for 50 years before it was accepted by the English people. It was the best English version in print for three centuries. Although Elizabethan English is more difficult for people to understand today, and the translation itself is not as accurate as newer ones, the language is elegant and pleasing to many. You might decide you want both the KJV and a contemporary version to study alongside it.

The **New Revised Standard Version** (NRSV), 1989, was updated from the **Revised Standard Version** (RSV) of 1952. The NRSV is a careful and accurate translation by a group of 30 respected scholars. It avoids archaic language and is inclusive when possible in referring to humans, although masculine references to God generally were kept. The RSV has been favored by many colleges and seminaries for study, and one might expect a similar response to the NRSV.

The **New International Version** (NIV), 1978, is a somewhat freer translation than the RSV. The language is contemporary and easy to understand. It is favored by those who once considered using only the KJV and is a leading seller, especially among more conservative Christians.

Today's English Version (TEV), 1977, also known as the Good News Version, is regarded by scholars as an accurate translation that avoids using less familiar English words. It is easy to read and is based on spoken rather than written language. TEV is an excellent choice for beginning Bible readers, as well as for children and youth.

Jerusalem Bible (JB), 1966, was translated into English from work done by French scholars and revised in 1985 (NJB). It is known for its extensive annotations and makes a good study Bible. Its literary quality is high, particularly in the poetry sections.

New English Bible (NEB), 1976, is known for literary accuracy and readability. It is the product of the Protestant churches in Great Britain. The translators sought to produce a text that is easy to understand without necessarily being word-for-word. The **Revised English Bible** (REB), 1990, attempts to remove some of the idiomatic British expressions of NEB.

The **Living Bible** (LB), 1971, is not a word-for-word translation but a paraphrase. The introduction says the purpose of the translation is "to say as exactly as possible what the writers of the Scriptures meant," but many scholars think too many passages are interpreted too freely. It has a conversational style and is usually recommended primarily for devotional reading.

When you select your Bible, do remember that there is no such thing as a perfect translation of the Bible. Besides being the Word of God, the Bible is also a human book. Our confidence in the Bible rests in the promise of God. By the work of the Holy Spirit, God will get through to us.

3 How to Study the Bible

Certainly you may begin your Bible reading by simply opening your Bible and choosing a section to read. But you will find that you learn and grow more if you have a plan or purpose for your reading.

There are a number of different ways to begin your study of the Bible. You might try several approaches before you find one that works for you. Or you might use two or three methods together. (Some of the study methods recommend using a Bible reference. See "Bible Helps and How to Use Them," page 15, for guidance.)

Study on Your Own

• Read select chapters to get a feel for various books of the Bible. See "One Hundred Most Important Chapters," page 23, for a list of chapters you could start with.

• Reading straight through the Bible in one year can be done by reading three chapters a day and five chapters on Sundays. If you set this as a goal, however, give yourself permission to slow down if you find that the pace prevents you from reading in a thoughtful manner.

• If there is a subject or story that particularly interests you, that is a good place to start. Locate stories or passages that might relate to the topic by using a concordance or Bible dictionary.

When you find passages that apply, you might want to write them down or just summarize the main ideas. Also note questions that come to mind and insights you have as you are reading.

■ Study an individual word that will lead you deeper into the text of the Bible. Start by reading passages that contain a significant word such as *faith, hope, love, compassion,* or *forgiveness.* See the section on the concordance, page 15, for help.

■ Explore life in Bible times to understand better the world in which biblical people lived. Think about how it would have been to live then. Use a Bible dictionary, atlas, or handbook.

Study with Others

■ Join a Bible study group. A group can be encouraging for those getting started. Each group member can contribute questions and insights to stimulate the group. A group offers the opportunity for mutual support in both faith and life.

■ If a class is not available, start one yourself. Talk to a pastor, teacher, bookstore clerk, or librarian to find out what kind of study materials are available. Ask two or three others to meet and discuss how you would like to proceed. You might take turns serving as discussion leader or as host. Consider inviting a resource person to sit in or to present a special study on occasion.

■ Many Bible students have a mentor or resource person to whom they go with questions. A pastor, church school teacher, or friend who has studied the Bible for several years might help you.

■ Offer to read the Bible in a church service or to open a meeting. Reading the Bible out loud can give you a better feel for the passage and increase your understanding of a passage.

How to Mark Your Bible

Whether you study alone or with others, marking your Bible will make it easy for you to return to familiar and important passages. You will better understand the Bible as you retrace your steps, finding more depth and beauty in God's Word.

You can highlight important passages or underline them with a ballpoint pen. You might prefer to write notes in the margin. Or you can use symbols to help you remember how a passage spoke to you. The following chart provides symbol suggestions:

SUGGESTED SYMBOLS	
(23)	Circle the number at the beginning of important chapters. (See page 23 for a list of important chapters.)
?	Something you do not understand appears here.
♡	God's love is revealed in this passage.
P	One of God's promises is given here.
✚	The passage describes a benefit of Jesus' death and resurrection.
HS	The work of the Holy Spirit is indicated here.
F	Faith, confidence, trust
H	Hope, perseverance, patience
↔	Interpersonal relationships, love, social concerns
P	Prayer
♪	Praise, joy, music, hymns
Rx	Strength, comfort, healing

You may, of course, make up your own symbols. It might be a good idea to list them on the inside cover of your study Bible.

How to Keep a Journal

Keeping a journal can be a satisfying way to record your thoughts and questions as you read the Bible. Write reflections that grow out of discussions or private study. You can review your thoughts and then make fresh applications.

Here is one way to start a journal:

Purchase a ring binder. A loose-leaf binder allows you to add or recopy and discard pages.

Set aside three or four pages for introductory and general information about the Bible. Then write the title of one book of the Bible in the upper right hand corner of each right hand page.

Using what you learn from this handbook and other resources, you might note for each book of the Bible basic information such as the number of chapters, key words, frequently quoted verses, and a brief outline. As you read material in that book, note your insights, reflections, questions, and personal experiences. Date your entries.

Other journal writing techniques might be helpful. For example, write a dialog between yourself and a key Bible character. Or imagine that you are in a situation described in a Bible passage, and write a description of the setting and your reactions. You can write prayers or letters to God. Or write a letter to another person who comes to mind when you read a passage. Always date your journal entries because when you look through your journal later, the date of your writing might tell you something important about how you responded to a passage at that time.

You do not need to write in your journal every day, and you need not write at length. You might write only the reference of the material you read. But a journal can become in effect a filing system and an important study companion.

4. How to Understand What You Read

Whether you read the Bible on your own or study with a group, begin your reading with a prayer, asking God to open your heart and mind to the promptings of the Holy Spirit. As you read, pay attention to the questions and insights that come to mind. There are also a few basic questions you can ask about the verses you are reading that will help you interpret what you read.

1. Who is being addressed by the passage? What are the person's or group's circumstances? What word needs to be heard in this situation? Ask yourself: How am I like or different from the person being addressed? What things that are said in the passage apply to me?

2. Does the text show you your need for God? What is the problem addressed? Does it also offer a remedy to help you overcome obstacles, grow in faith, forgive, or share your faith? These questions help distinguish Law and Gospel. God speaks in two ways: God judges and God shows mercy. The Law shows us our need for God, God's judgment. The Gospel shows us God's response to our need, God's mercy.

3. What type of literature is the passage? Is it poetry? A parable? A sermon? A historical account? A hymn? How might that shape your understanding of the passage?

4. How does the passage relate to the surrounding text (perhaps the rest of the chapter or even the entire book)? Does the surrounding material shed any light on the passage's meaning?

5. How does the passage compare to parallel passages or other texts on the same subject? Does another text clarify the passage?

6. Is there any doubt about the clear meaning of the passage? Do you need to check references for further explanation? (See "Bible Helps and How to Use Them," page 15.) There are a few mystifying paragraphs and obscure verses, but most of the Bible is quite clear. Mark Twain once remarked, "It is not the parts of the Bible that I don't understand that bother me; what bothers me are the parts I do understand."

End your study by reflecting on the question, "How do I apply God's Word in my everyday living?" It is when we *live* God's Word that we truly come to understand it. On the basis of his study of Psalm 119, a psalm about God's Word, the reformer Martin Luther recommended that a person first pray over the Word, then think and meditate about what it says, and finally try that Word out in the tensions of life. Then we begin to understand. And as our lives change, and we continue to read and reread Scripture, we discover more about even the most familiar passages of Scripture. The Bible proves itself to be an unending resource for faith and life. The Bible satisfies our hunger for God.

5 Bible Helps and How to Use Them

As you read the Bible, expect to have questions about the text. And know that finding your way through the Bible can be a daunting job for anyone. But be assured, too, that there are many excellent references to help a person. Here is an overview of the most common types of helps.

Reference materials, short versions of the materials described below, are printed in the back of some Bibles. The references are printed as separate volumes, however, and cover their topics more extensively.

An **annotated or study Bible** typically contains introductions to the books of the Bible; brief outlines of the books; notes on difficult verses or words; chapter outlines; and articles of general interest on history and geography, translations, and Bible study methods.

The best commentary on the Bible is often a text from another part of the Bible. Therefore, it is often helpful to check the **cross-references**. A cross-reference lists a Bible verse followed by references to one or more related or similar verses. Study Bibles have the most important cross-references listed either in a center column or at the bottom of the page. Cross-references are also known as parallel passages.

A **concordance** helps you locate a Bible passage when you know only a word or a phrase from the verse. There are separate concordances for each major translation of the Bible. Find one written for your Bible's translation. To use a concordance, look up a key word from the passage you want to find. Following the word will be a list of verses, along with the portion of each passage that includes the key word.

For example, to find the verse that starts "God so loved the world . . .," look up *world*. Notice that the Bible verses are listed in the order they appear in the Bible. Scan the verses. After John 3:16 you will find the phrase, "God so loved the *w*." You can look up the passage, explore the surrounding text, and check cross-references. When you decide which word to look up, choose one that is important in the verse but not too common. In this case, for example, you would not look up *God* or *love* because there would be too many references to review easily.

A concordance also helps you do a word study. By checking many references that include the same word, you can explore the way that word is used in the Bible. Often a passage becomes clearer when a key word is understood in a new light.

A **commentary** includes the biblical text plus a verse-by-verse explanation of the Bible. A commentary provides more detail than a study Bible. There are one-volume commentaries on the entire Bible, as well as commentaries with separate volumes for individual books of the Bible.

Handbooks of the Bible do not reprint the text of the Bible, but the articles, which can be extensive, follow the order of the Bible.

A **Bible dictionary** contains short articles on words and topics such as people named in the Bible, groups such as the Pharisees, geography and history, culture, animals, and rituals.

An **atlas** of the Bible, often included in another reference book, provides maps of Bible lands at various periods of history. You might find helpful a map of Bible lands that prints both the current and ancient names of places.

6 What Is in the Bible?

Many religious writings tell of humanity's search for God. From beginning to end, the Bible tells the story of God's search for humankind. Christians believe God speaks to us in ways we can understand. The Bible tells of God's repeated efforts to establish a personal relationship with us. From a historic perspective, three major events are described and repeatedly referred to in the Bible:

The Exodus: Israelites had gone to Egypt to escape famine in their own land. Many settled there, and later they became slaves of the Egyptian rulers, the pharaohs. The deliverance of the children of Israel from Egypt in 1200 B.C. is called the exodus. Led by Moses, the Israelites wandered in the wilderness for 40 years. God gave Moses the Commandments at Mt. Sinai.

The Exile: Gradually the people of Israel became a nation and later a divided nation. Often the land was overrun by other more powerful nations, and in 586 B.C. the tiny kingdom of Judah was attacked by mighty Babylon. The nation's 70 years of captivity in Babylon is called the exile.

The Christ Event: The life, death, and resurrection of Jesus took place in the years up to about A.D. 30. But this event is still in progress, moving toward Christ's return at the end of time.

There are 66 books in the Bible, 39 in the Old Testament and 27 in the New Testament. Below are brief descriptions of the books of the

Bible. Eighteen of the more frequently read books are marked with an asterisk. Try reading first Mark's gospel and Genesis, or portions of the Psalms in the Old Testament. Then continue your study by reading several of the other more familiar books.

The Old Testament

*The Pentateuch (Five Books)
or the Torah (Instruction)*

***Genesis**   The first book tells the stories of the creation of the world, the entry of sin into the world, and the flood. Several people of faith, including Abraham and Sarah and their descendants, are introduced.

***Exodus**   Moses leads the descendants or children of Israel from Egypt, and they begin their journey to Canaan, the promised land.

Leviticus   This book is a manual for priests, who instruct Israel in ritual and social law.

Numbers   The Israelites are counted, or numbered, during their 40-year sojourn in the wilderness.

***Deuteronomy**   The law given in Exodus is given again and reinterpreted.

The Historical Books

Joshua   The conquest of Canaan under Moses' successor, Joshua, begins with the siege of Jericho.

Judges   Tribal heroes like Deborah, Gideon, and Samson lead military expeditions and govern Israel until the time of Samuel.

Ruth   Ruth, devoted to her mother-in-law, Naomi, moves to Naomi's homeland. There she meets and marries Boaz. Ruth was an ancestor of King David.

1 and 2 Samuel   Samuel, the last of the
judges and first of the prophets, anoints the first
two kings of the monarchy, Saul and David.

1 and 2 Kings   Approximately 400 years of
history are covered from the glorious reign of
Solomon and the building of the Temple to the
beginning of the exile in 586 B.C.

1 and 2 Chronicles   The eras of David and
Solomon are described, with special interest in the
kingdom of Judah.

Ezra and Nehemiah   Some of the Israelites
return from exile and work to restore their nation.

Esther   Like a story out of *Arabian Nights*,
Queen Esther saves her people during the exile.

Wisdom Literature

Job   Job and his friends talk about whether
suffering is always caused by sin and whether sin
is always punished. Job continues in his faith
toward God.

***Psalms**   These prayers and hymns express deep
emotion, from despair to highest praise.

Proverbs   Love and trust for the Lord is the
beginning of wisdom. This book offers advice on
everything from personal morals to business.

Ecclesiastes   An older preacher-philosopher
reflects on the futility of various pursuits and
finally determines that life is worth living.

Song of Solomon   This series of love songs is
sometimes interpreted to symbolize the love
between God and his people.

The Major Prophets

***Isaiah**   The longest and greatest prophecy, Isaiah
is bright with hope for the returning exiles.

Jeremiah   This passionate prophet agonizes over

the last days of Jerusalem and the beginning of its captivity.

Lamentations This book is a collection of poetic laments over the fall of Jerusalem.

Ezekiel An extraordinarily versatile prophet-priest-visionary-organizer keeps hope alive during the exile.

Daniel A man of wisdom, prayer, and great faith survives under the rule of foreign powers.

The Minor Prophets

Hosea A compassionate prophet, Hosea despairs over Israel and proclaims God's faithfulness.

Joel Joel says God will judge the people, but there also will be a pouring out of God's Spirit.

Amos Amos sometimes is considered the social reformer of the Old Testament.

Obadiah Israel's enemy, Edom, is condemned.

Jonah Colorful Jonah does not want to preach repentance in Nineveh as God wants him to.

Micah God calls for justice and offers hope.

Nahum Nahum cries in outrage over Nineveh, for three centuries the scourge of the Middle East.

Habakkuk Habakkuk asks why evil is allowed to persist and yet holds on to faith.

Zephaniah Zephaniah is sometimes called the Old Testament prophet of fire.

Haggai, Zechariah, and Malachi Three prophets from the period after the exile try to rebuild the people's hope.

The New Testament

The Four Gospels

***Matthew** Written for a Greek-speaking Jewish community, yet with a universal outlook, Matthew builds the case that Jesus was the promised Messiah.

***Mark** The shortest of the Gospels, Mark was written earliest. He reports reactions of people to Jesus, whose purpose is revealed only gradually.

***Luke** Written as instruction in the faith, Luke describes Jesus as a compassionate benefactor.

***John** John focuses on the deity of Christ and is more abstract than the other evangelists. John says he writes "that you may believe that Jesus is the Christ" (John 20:31).

Historical Book

***Acts** Possibly written by the same person who wrote Luke, Acts describes the work of the Holy Spirit in the establishment of the Christian church from Jerusalem to Rome.

Letters from Paul

***Romans** Paul explains to Roman Christians the power of the gospel for everyone who believes, Jew and Gentile alike.

***1 and 2 Corinthians** These two pastoral letters to the church at Corinth reveal a church divided and full of problems, yet also filled with many gifts.

***Galatians** This letter sets a course between legalism and liberty, and counsels the Galatians to depend on faith and not their own works.

***Ephesians** Paul assures the Ephesians that God's goals for the church are great.

***Philippians** In the warmest of Paul's letters to his favorite congregation, Paul emphasizes the joy of giving and receiving from one another in Christ.

Colossians Paul exalts Christ and affirms God's rule in an effort to challenge various heresies.

1 and 2 Thessalcnians   Perhaps the earliest of Paul's letters, these are addressed to Christians who expected Christ's immediate return to earth and offer encouragement to the young community.

Pastoral Letters

1 and 2 Timothy and Titus   Paul advises two of his delegates to minister to the household of God with doctrine grounded in the gospel.

Philemon   Paul appeals to Philemon to take back a runaway slave, Onesimus.

General Letters

Hebrews   The writer exhorts Jewish converts to keep their eyes fixed on Jesus, the pioneer and perfecter of faith.

James   Probably written when the church was young and mostly Jewish, this letter stresses the importance of an active faith.

***1 and 2 Peter**   These short letters touch on a variety of themes. They provide instructions and encouragement to Christians in several communities.

***1, 2, and 3 John**   The first letter exposes false teachers and assures believers of salvation. The other two letters urge support for teachers of the gospel.

Jude   Much like 2 Peter, this letter urges recipients to be wary of false teachers.

***Revelation**   Written as the church was entering a time of persecution, Revelation uses highly symbolic language to encourage Christians to resist emperor worship. It also warns readers that there will be a final conflict between God and Satan.

7 One Hundred Most Important Chapters

Of the 1,189 chapters in the Bible, about 100 chapters have been turned to most often for inspiration and direction. Those chapters and parallel or related chapters are listed below.

You might like to circle the numbers of these chapters in your Bible. The circles will serve as reminders to you in your travels through Scripture: slow down, important, investigate further.

You also might want to find a few chapters that are especially meaningful for you. Study them further. Write about them in your journal. Let them become your companions through the years.

In the Beginning

Genesis 1, 2	The creation (also Psalm 104)
Genesis 3	The fall into sin (also John 3; Romans 5)
Genesis 6, 7	Noah and the flood
Genesis 17	God's covenant with Abraham (also Romans 4)
Genesis 22	God's test of Abraham's faith
Exodus 3, 4	God's call to Moses
Exodus 12	The first Passover
Exodus 20	The Ten Commandments (also Deuteronomy 6)

The Psalms: A Book of Devotions

Psalm 8	God's name is majestic
Psalm 19	Creation and law reveal God

Psalm 22	Has God forsaken me?
Psalm 23	The Lord is my shepherd (also John 10)
Psalm 27	God is my strength
Psalm 30	Rejoicing comes in the morning
Psalm 32	Blessed are the forgiven
Psalm 51	Create in me a pure heart, O God
Psalm 71	God is my refuge
Psalm 84	God's dwelling place
Psalm 90	God is our dwelling place
Psalm 91	God will bear you up
Psalm 95	Sing to the Lord
Psalm 100	Shout for joy to the Lord
Psalm 103	Praise the Lord, O my soul
Psalm 119	God's word is my lamp
Psalm 121	I lift up my eyes to the hills
Psalm 130	Out of the depths I cry
Psalm 139	God searches and knows me
Psalm 145	God cares for all creation

Wisdom Literature

Job 38, 39	Nature reveals God's profound wisdom
Proverbs 1, 8, 9	An invitation to wisdom
Ecclesiastes 3	For everything there is a season

The Voice of Prophecy

Isaiah 6	God's call to Isaiah
Isaiah 40	Comfort for God's people
Isaiah 55	God's universal call
Isaiah 61	The mission of the Messiah
Jeremiah 31	The new covenant
Ezekiel 37	The valley of dry bones

Daniel 6	Daniel in the lion's den

The Life of Jesus

John 1	The Word became flesh
Luke 2	The birth of Jesus
Matthew 2	The coming of the Magi
Matthew 3	Jesus' baptism (also Mark 1; Luke 3; John 1)
Matthew 4	Jesus' temptation (Mark 1; Luke 4)
Mark 9	Jesus' transfiguration (also Matthew 17; Luke 9)
Matthew 21	Jesus' entry into Jerusalem
John 18, 19	Jesus' suffering and crucifixion (also Matthew 26, 27; Mark 14, 15; Luke 22, 23)
Luke 24	The resurrection (also Matthew 28; Mark 16; John 20)
Acts 1	The ascension (also Luke 24)

Jesus' Teaching

John 3	God so loved the world (also Romans 5; 1 Corinthians 15)
Matthew 5, 6, 7	The Sermon on the Mount
Matthew 10	The sending of the Twelve
Matthew 13	Parables of the kingdom
John 6	The Bread of Life
John 10	The Good Shepherd (also Psalm 23; Ezekiel 34)
Luke 10	The good Samaritan
Luke 15	Parables of the lost and found
Matthew 25	Our talents and our time
John 14	Comfort for the disciples
John 15	The vine and the branches

The Faith

John 14	The work of the Holy Spirit
Acts 2	The day of Pentecost
Romans 3, 4, 5	Justification through faith (also Galatians 2, 3)
1 Corinthians 1	The scandal of the cross
Romans 12	Members of the body of Christ
Romans 14, 15	The strong and the weak
1 Corinthians 12	The church as the body of Christ
Ephesians 4	The church's unity
Ephesians 5	The church as bride of Christ
Ephesians 6	The whole armor of God
Hebrews 12	Perseverance in the race before us

The Last Times

Mark 13	The little revelation of Jesus
1 Corinthians 15	The resurrection of the body
Revelation 5, 7	A vision of the throne and the Lamb
Revelation 21	A vision of new heaven and earth

Three Characteristics of a Christian

Hebrews 11, 12	Faith (also Romans 3; Galatians 2)
Romans 7, 8	Hope
1 Corinthians 13	Love (also 1 John 4)

Sayings of Jesus

During Jesus' earthly ministry, his mother, the disciples, Jesus' enemies, religious and civil leaders, and the crowds that heard him all recognized and were amazed that Jesus spoke with great authority. There are about 35,000 words in the Bible attributed to Jesus. Here are some of the most quoted sayings of Jesus:

Matthew 4:4	Man does not live on bread alone
Matthew 5:3-10	The Beatitudes: Blessed are the poor in spirit . . .
Matthew 5:13	You are the salt of the earth
Matthew 5:14	You are the light of the world
Matthew 5:16	Let your light shine before others
Matthew 6:9-13	"Our Father in heaven " . . .
Matthew 6:20-21	Store up for yourselves treasures in heaven
Matthew 6:24	No one can serve two masters
Matthew 6:33-34	Seek first his kingdom
Matthew 7:12	Do to others what you would have them do to you
Matthew 10:30	Even the very hairs of your head are all numbered
Matthew 11:28	Come to me, all you who are weary

Matthew 16:15-19	I will give you keys of the kingdom
Matthew 18:20	Where two or three come together in my name
Matthew 19:24	It is easier for a camel to go through the eye of a needle
Matthew 19:30	Many who are first will be last . . .
Matthew 22:21	Give to Caesar what is Caesar's
Matthew 22:34-40	This is the first and greatest commandment
Matthew 25:21	Well done, good and faithful servant
Matthew 25:31-46	I was hungry and you gave me something to eat
Matthew 26:26-29	This is my body . . . this is my blood
Matthew 26:39	Father, if it is possible, may this cup be taken from me
Matthew 27:46	My God, my God, why have you forsaken me?
Matthew 28:18-20	Therefore go and make disciples
Mark 1:15	Repent and believe the good news
Mark 1:17	Come, follow me
Mark 10:14	Let the little children come to me
Mark 10:27	All things are possible with God
Mark 10:45	The Son of Man [came] . . . to give his life as a ransom
Mark 13:31	My words will never pass away

Mark 14:38	Watch and pray
Luke 9:23-27	Take up your cross
Luke 11:9-13	Ask . . . seek . . . knock
Luke 17:4	Seven times . . . forgive him
Luke 23:34	Father, forgive them
Luke 23:43	Today you will be with me in paradise
Luke 23:46	Father, into your hands I commit my spirit
John 3:7	You must be born again
John 3:16-17	God so loved the world
John 8:12	I am the light of the world
John 8:31-32	The truth will set you free
John 10:11	I am the good shepherd
John 11:25	I am the resurrection and the life
John 13:34	A new command I give you: Love one another
John 14:6	I am the way and the truth and the life
John 14:27	Peace I leave with you
John 15:5	I am the vine; you are the branches
John 18:36	My kingdom is not of this world
John 19:26-27	Woman, here is your son
John 19:28	I am thirsty
John 19:30	It is finished
John 20:21	Peace be with you
John 20:29	Blessed are those who have not seen and yet have believed

9 Where to Find Passages in Time of Need

When seeking direction
Psalm 23 ▪ The Lord is my shepherd

When feeling troubled and alone
John 10:11, 14-16, 27-28 ▪ The good shepherd
lays down his life for the sheep
Psalm 139 ▪ O Lord, you have searched me and
you know me

When under stress
Psalm 42 ▪ As the deer pants for water
Romans 7:15—8:1 ▪ I do not understand what I
do . . . it is sin living in me

When the future looks bleak
Romans 8:28, 31-39 ▪ God works for the good
of those who love him

When conscience-stricken
1 Corinthians 4:2-5 ▪ I do not even judge myself.
My conscience is clear . . .
1 John 3:19-23 ▪ God is greater than our hearts,
and he knows everything
Psalm 51:10-12 ▪ Create in me a pure heart

When afraid
Psalm 27 ▪ The Lord is my light . . . whom shall
I fear?
John 14:27 ▪ Peace I leave with you

When really low
Psalm 130 ▪ Out of the depths I cry to you

Under all circumstances
Ecclesiastes 3:1-15 ▪ There is a time for everything . . . a time to be born and to die

Philippians 4:4-13 ▪ I can do everything through
    him who gives me strength

For protection
Psalm 91 ▪ He is my refuge and my fortress

For patience
1 Corinthians 13:4-7 ▪ Love is patient
Isaiah 40:31 ▪ Those who hope in the Lord will
    renew their strength

For perseverance
Hebrews 12:1-3 ▪ Let us run with perseverance
James 5:11 ▪ You have heard of Job's persever-
    ance and . . . what the Lord brought about

When thankful
Psalm 30 ▪ You turned my wailing into dancing
Psalm 103 ▪ Praise the Lord, O my soul

For comfort in time of sorrow
John 14:1-9a, 18-19 ▪ Because I live, you also
    will live
1 Corinthians 15:51-58 ▪ Listen, I tell you a
    mystery . . . we will all be changed

Bibliography

A Beginner's Guide to the Books of the Bible. Minneapolis: Augsburg Fortress, 1991.

A Beginner's Guide to Reading the Bible. Minneapolis: Augsburg Fortress, 1991.

A Beginner's Guide to Studying the Bible. Minneapolis: Augsburg Fortress, 1991.

Concordia Self-Study Bible. New International Version. St. Louis: Concordia Publishing House, 1986.

Harper's Bible Commentary. San Francisco: Harper & Row, 1988.

Harper's Bible Dictionary. San Francisco: Harper & Row, 1985.

Harper Study Bible. Revised Standard Version. Grand Rapids: Zondervan Publishing House, 1965.

The Interpreter's Dictionary of the Bible. Nashville: Abingdon Press, 1962.

The Interpreter's One-Volume Commentary on the Bible. Nashville: Abingdon Press, 1971.

New Oxford Annotated Bible. New Revised Standard Version. New York: Oxford University Press, 1991.

New Oxford Annotated Bible. Revised Standard Version. New York: Oxford University Press, 1973.

Oxford NIV Scofield Study Bible. New York: Oxford University Press, 1967.